A QUICK INTRODUCTION TO THE AFRICAN CONTINENT

Geography Books for Kids Age 9-12
Children's Geography & Cultures Books

BABY PROFESSOR

EDUCATION KIDS

Speedy Publishing LLC

40 E. Main St. #1156

Newark, DE 19711

www.speedypublishing.com

Copyright 2017

In this book, we're going to cover an introduction to the African continent's geography and highlights from some of its many countries. So let's get right to it!

THE WATERS SURROUNDING AFRICA

At over 11.7 million square miles (30.3 square kilometers), the continent of Africa is the second largest continent in terms of land-mass. It's surrounded by bodies of water on all four sides. The Mediterranean Sea is at its northern border and this is the body of water that separates it from Europe. It is separated from the continent of Asia by the Red Sea and the Suez Canal.

On its west coast is the mighty Atlantic Ocean and on its east the Indian Ocean surrounds it. This massive continent is also the second most populated continent. The equator divides its landmass almost exactly in half. The hottest of all seven continents, Africa has eight major regions

including the Sahel, the transition area from the Sahara desert in the north to the southern savannas, the Sahara desert, the savannas, the rainforest, the highlands of Ethiopia, the Swahili coast and the Great Lakes of Africa and Southern Africa.

Sahara Desert

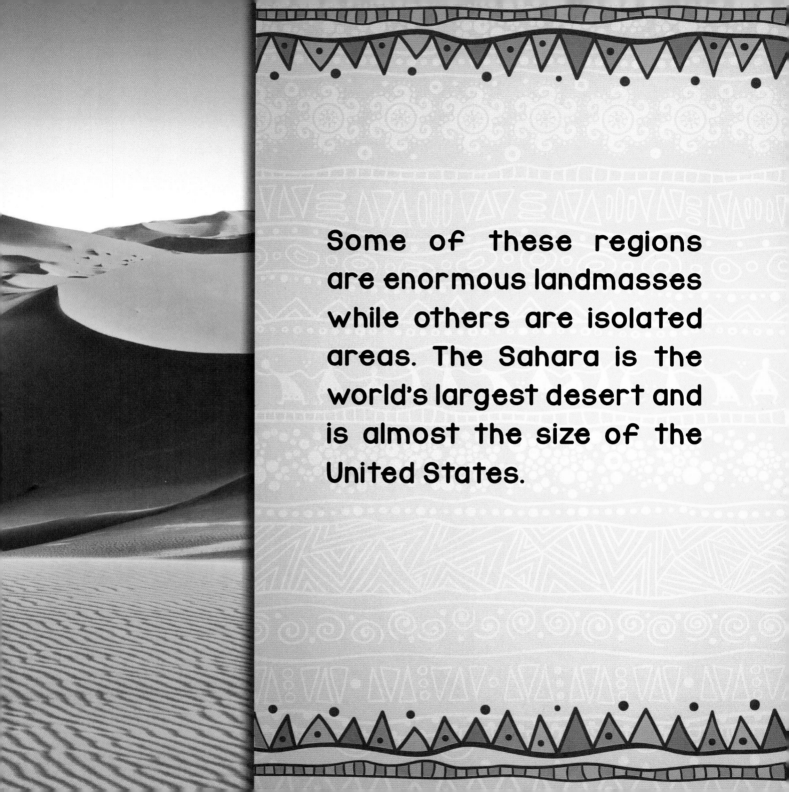

Some of these regions are enormous landmasses while others are isolated areas. The Sahara is the world's largest desert and is almost the size of the United States.

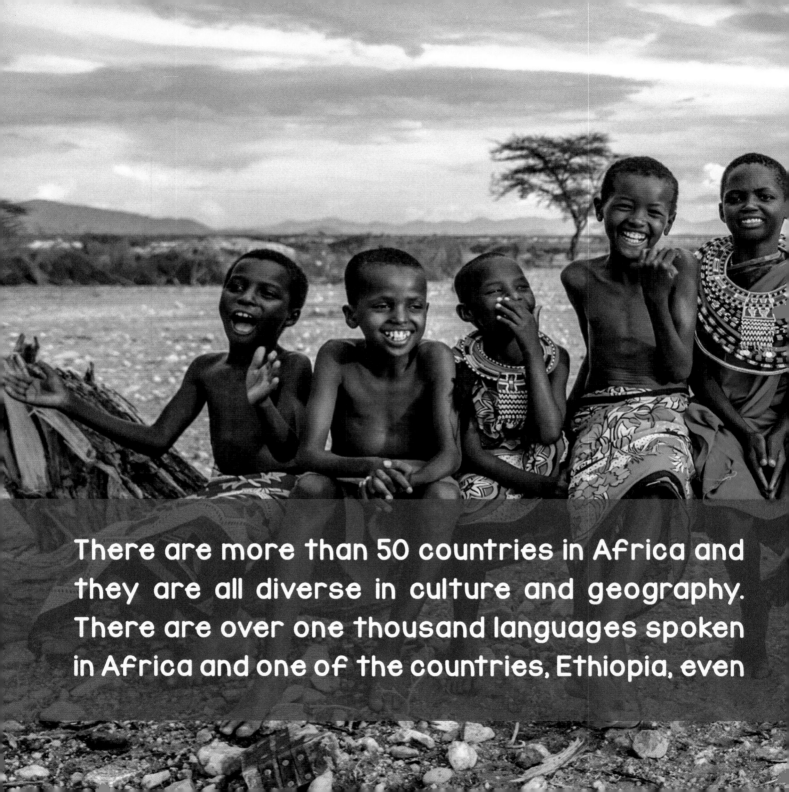

There are more than 50 countries in Africa and they are all diverse in culture and geography. There are over one thousand languages spoken in Africa and one of the countries, Ethiopia, even

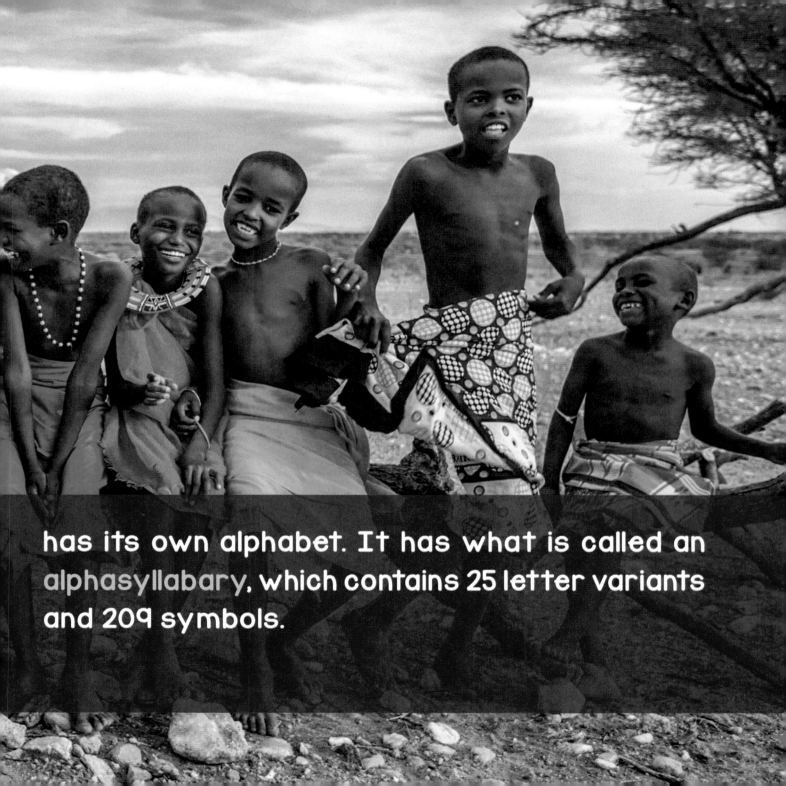

has its own alphabet. It has what is called an alphasyllabary, which contains 25 letter variants and 209 symbols.

GEOGRAPHICAL FEATURES OF THE CONTINENT

The highest mountain peak in Africa is Mount Kilimanjaro. It rises over 19,300 feet (5,883 meters). Even though it's close to the equator, it has glaciers on its peak since it's so high in the atmosphere. Victoria Falls is the tallest waterfall in Africa and Lake Victoria is the largest lake and the source of the mighty Nile River.

Mount Kilimanjaro

THE ANIMALS OF AFRICA

Africa is known for its amazing wildlife. It's home to the largest land animal, the African elephant, and it's also home to the tallest animal, the giraffe. The fastest land animal in the world, the cheetah, is also native to Africa.

Africa has the largest reptile in the world, which is the Nile crocodile, as well as the largest primate in the world, which is the gorilla. Our ancestors also started in Africa.

The oldest human remains ever found were discovered in Ethiopia. They have been dated to approximately 200,000 years old.

HIGHLIGHTS OF SOME OF AFRICA'S FASCINATING COUNTRIES

Africa has over 50 countries. Algeria is the largest country, but Nigeria is the country that's the most populated. The smallest country in Africa is the Seychelles, which is a group of 115 islands located northeast of Madagascar.

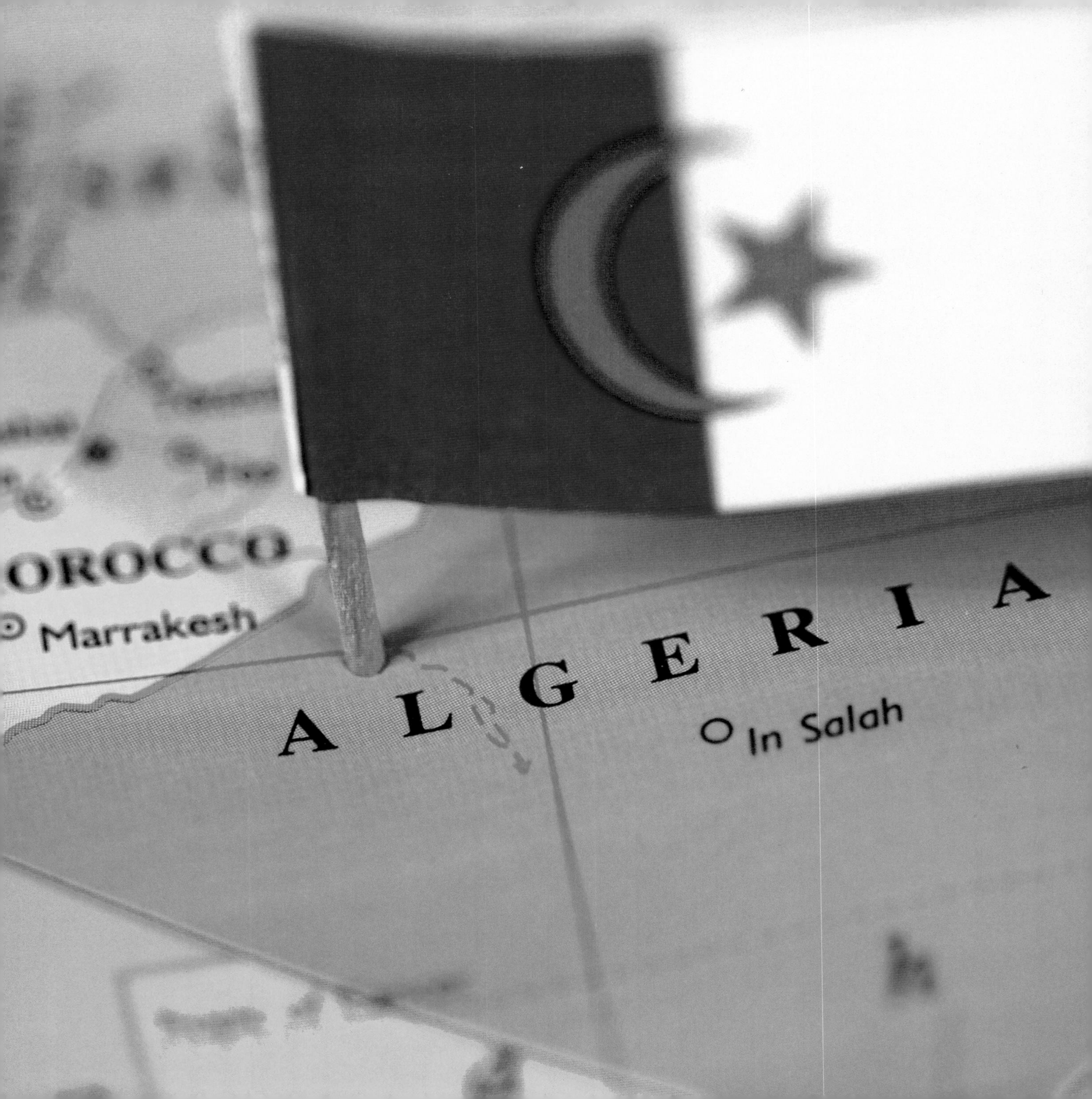

OROCCO
Marrakesh
ALGERIA
In Salah

ALGERIA

Over 90% of the country of Algeria is covered by the Sahara desert. It's the largest country in Africa in terms of landmass, but only 12% of its land is inhabited. One of the notable places in Algeria is the city of Djemila, the remains of the ancient Roman town of Cuicul. This archaeological wonder was excavated prior to 1957 but there is still much work to be done there.

Many fine mosaics and statues have been uncovered and there are wonderful examples of the usual civic Roman structures, such as baths, a forum, a triumphal arch, a theatre, a market, and various temples. The beautiful buildings were integrated into the mountain landscape.

Buildings on a Mountain Landscape

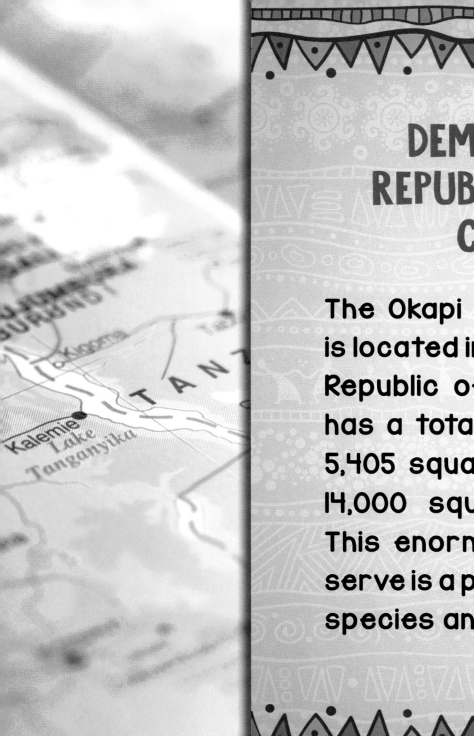

DEMOCRATIC REPUBLIC OF THE CONGO

The Okapi Wildlife Reserve is located in the Democratic Republic of the Congo. It has a total area of nearly 5,405 square miles, almost 14,000 square kilometers. This enormous wildlife reserve is a paradise for plant species and wildlife.

Over 50 different mammal species have natural habitats there including the unusual okapi, which is a relative of the giraffe, the African golden cat, elephants, crocodiles, leopards, chimpanzees, forest buffalo, and many others.

Okapi

EGYPT

Although Egypt is located geographically in Africa, it is considered to be part of the Middle East. Along the Nile River Valley, the colossal pyramids of Giza and the Great Sphinx still exist although they were built thousands of years ago.

ETHIOPIA

The legendary Ark of the Covenant, once in Solomon's temple in Jerusalem, is said to be housed in a church in the country. Only one monk, the ark's official guardian, is allowed to see and be in the room with the Ark. Because of this protocol, no one really knows if it is housed there or not.

Canopy Walkway

GHANA

The Kakum National Park in Ghana is known for its canopy walkway that is 30 meters above the forest floor. It's within sight of the forest's tallest tree where elephants sometimes grab fallen fruit. The park has over 250 species of native birds including African grey and Senegal parrots. Over 500 species of butterflies also live in the park and a new species was found there in 1993.

KENYA

Both Tanzania and Kenya are home to one of the largest mammal migrations in the world. Every year, the great wildebeest migration starts in December in the southern Serengeti plains of Tanzania.

Wildebeests

There are rich grasslands for feeding during this time and 750,000 zebra followed by 1.2 million wildebeest travel 500 miles (800 kilometers) to the Maasai Mara Reserve in Kenya.

Kenya only has two seasons a year, a rainy season and a dry season. Another interesting fact about Kenya is that even though one of its biggest exports is coffee, most of its citizens drink tea!

MOROCCO

Even though Morocco is in Africa, it's only 8 miles (13 kilometers) from Europe across the Strait of Gibraltar. Morocco is known for its souks, which are stalls in the marketplaces filled with aromatic spices from around the world.

Hassan II Mosque

The Hassan II Mosque in Casablanca, Morocco is the seventh largest mosque in the world. It took 30,000 workers and five years of intense labor to complete the mosque finally in 1993. In terms of covered area, it is the largest mosque worldwide and has enough space for over 80,000 worshippers.

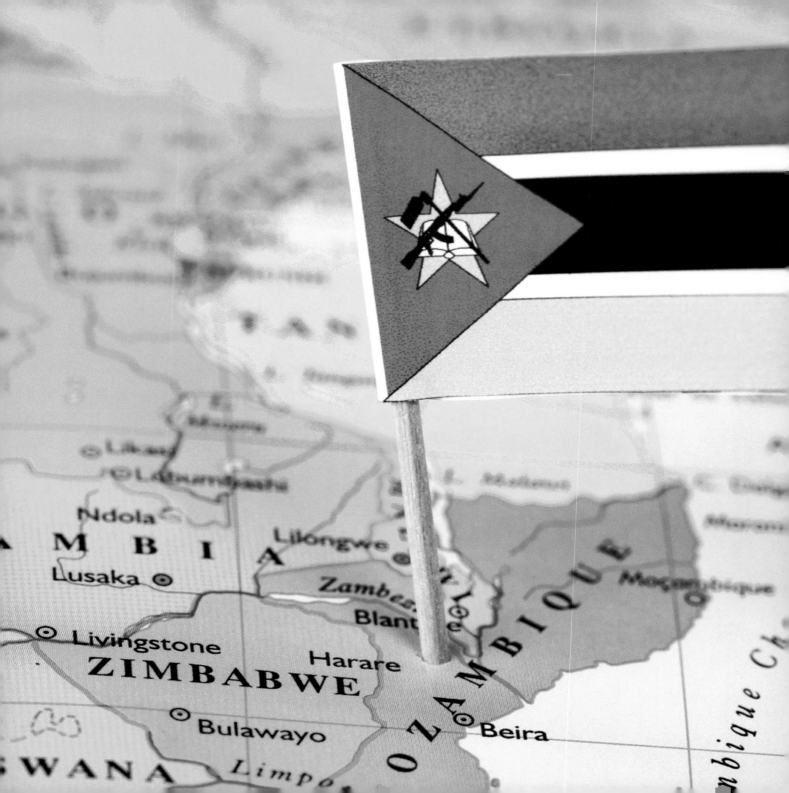

MOZAMBIQUE

An important feature of Mozambique is its long coastline facing the Indian Ocean. The coast has popular beaches like Tofo as well as offshore marine parks, such as Quirimbas Marine National Park in the Quirimbas Archipelago. These thirty-four coral islands cover a stretch of 155 miles (250 kilometers).

They are linked to the coast by sand bars, coral reefs, mangroves, and clear water with abundant marine life. The islands feature old Swahili settlements as well as settlements from the era when Portugal ruled Mozambique. Bottlenose dolphins, humpback dolphins, and whales breed in the coast's waters.

Mozambique Coastline

NIGERIA

The country of Nigeria is known for its amazing wildlife reserves. Cross River National Park and Yankari National Park have gorgeous waterfalls, dense rainforests, sprawling savannas, and unique primate habitats. The large monolith called Zuma Rock is a symbol of Nigeria and is pictured on its currency.

SOUTH AFRICA

The country of South Africa is home to the Kruger National Park one of the world's largest wildlife sanctuaries. Within its untamed environment, about the land area of the country of Wales, there are chances to see the animals that are nicknamed "the Big 5": elephants, rhinoceros, leopards, lions, and cape buffaloes. Over a million people come annually to view the wildlife in this isolated, protected reserve.

A geographic wonder of South Africa, Table
Mountain was formed by rocks that were
deposited by an ancient glacier hundreds of
millions of years ago.

It's 3,563 feet (1086 meters) above sea level at its highest point and can be seen from 124 miles (200 kilometers) out at sea.

SUDAN

The coastline of the Red Sea is one of Sudan's most beautiful natural wonders. The clear water, intricate coral reefs, such as Sanganeb and Shub Rumi, and the marine gardens are a haven for scuba divers.

UGANDA

Located in southwestern Uganda at the edge of the Rift Valley is Bwindi Impenetrable National Park. Its misty hillsides are covered by a rainforest that dates back over 25,000 years. Its fame is due to the fact that roughly half of the world's endangered mountain gorillas live there.

Mountain gorilla living in
Bwindi Impenetrable National Park

Several of the mountain gorilla families have been habituated, which means that humans can interact with them and learn more about their behavior. Uganda is also known for the world's best mangoes, bananas, pineapples, and avocados.

UNITED REPUBLIC OF TANZANIA

Tanzania is the home of the tallest mountain in Africa, Mount Kilimanjaro. This majestic mountain is the tallest free-standing mountain worldwide. The peak of Uhuru is its highest point at 19,340 feet (5895 meters). The world's earliest human skull was found in Tanzania in the Olduvai Gorge.

ONGRATULATIONS
YOU ARE NOW AT
AK, TANZANIA 5895M AMSL
S HIGHEST POINT
HIGHEST FREE-STANDING M

Awesome! Now you know more about the amazing continent of Africa. You can find more Geography and Cultures books from Baby Professor by searching the website of your favorite book retailer.

Visit

BABY PROFESSOR
EDUCATION KIDS

www.BabyProfessorBooks.com

to download Free Baby Professor eBooks
and view our catalog of new and exciting
Children's Books

Made in the USA
Coppell, TX
16 May 2020